ECOUTEZ BIEN 2

Leavin Certificate

Listening Comprehension Tests

SECOND EDITION REVISED

Student's Book

Joseph Dunne M.A., H.D.E.

FOLENS

Acknowledgements

The author wishes to acknowledge and thank the large number of French speakers who helped with the recording of the cassettes and CDs.

Editor
Margaret Burns

Design and Layout
Paula Byrne

Artist
Lynne Reece Loftus

ISBN 978-1-84131-854-7

Folens Publishers,
Hibernian Industrial Estate,
Greenhills Road,
Tallaght,
Dublin 24.

Preface

Ecoutez Bien 2 provides students with suitable and adequate aural practice for the Leaving Certificate Examination – where the Listening Comprehension section accounts for a significant proportion of the marks (20% at Higher Level, 25% at Ordinary Level).

Ecoutez Bien 2 consists of four elements:
- A Student's Book, containing the questions
- A Teacher's Tapescript
- Two audio cassette tapes
- Two CDs (provided with the Student's Book)

The cassettes and the CDs contain all the recorded material.

A large number of native French speakers (adults and teenagers) has been used in the studio recordings to add variety and authenticity to the material.

Joseph Dunne
2004

Table des matières

1. Mon premier emploi

Cédrine has managed to find her dream job.

1. What age is Cédrine?..

2. What type of *baccalauréat* will she be sitting? ....

3. She says that she would like to continue her studies at university.

   True ☐   False ☐

4. When did she see the advertisement in the newspaper? ....

★   ★   ★

5. The successful applicant for one of these jobs with *Look Voyages*

   (a) should be interested in sport

   (b) should be artistic

   (c) should be aged between 18 and 25

   (d) should be willing to train for two months in Britain

   Which one of these statements is **not** true?

   Write (a), (b), (c) or (d) in the box.   ☐

6. Where are the holiday clubs situated? *(three details)*

    (i)..

    (ii)...

    (iii)..

★ ★ ★

7. Where did the interview take place? ....

8. Why is Cédrine particularly pleased to have got this job?

    ....

2. On va déménager

Christian explains why his family has decided to move house.

1. What age is Christian? ....

2. What is he studying?..

3. On which floor is their apartment? ....

4. What comment does he make about the lift?...

★   ★   ★

5. How far from the city-centre do they live?...

6. What are the two major difficulties that he mentions regarding living in this apartment?

    (i)..

    (ii)...

★   ★   ★

7. When is the family going to move to their new home? ....

8. Write down two of the advantages that living in this new home will bring:

    (i)..

    (ii)...

9. How will Christian earn some money? ....

3. Les informations

You will hear three news items and a sports result.

1. First news item

1. Where in France did these floods occur? ....

2. How many people were forced to leave their homes? ....

3. To pump the water, the rescue services needed

    (a) 240 trucks

    (b) 800 firemen

    (c) assistance from three other countries

    (d) all the firemen in France

    Write (a), (b), (c) or (d) in the box.

4. How many businesses have been affected? ....

★ ★ ★

2. Second news item

1. By what percentage have cigarette sales fallen? ....

2. Sales of cigars have also shown a slight decrease.

    True [ ]   False [ ]

★ ★ ★

3. Third news item

1. What have people been told not to pick?

   (a) Wild mushrooms

   (b) Shellfish

   (c) Snails

   (d) Berries

   Write (a), (b), (c) or (d) in the box.

2. Why has it been necessary to introduce this ban?

   ....

   ★　★　★

4. Sport

1. Which team did Lorient defeat?..

2. What was the score?..

3. What happened before the end of the game?.......................................

des inondations

quitter leur domicile

des barques

les rues sont noyées

les dégâts

chez les buralistes

les zones littorales

Lorient porte plainte

4. La météo

You will hear the weather forecast for the following day in four French regions.

1. Mediterranean – Corsica

   1. What will the weather be like?...

   2. What temperatures are predicted for the afternoon? ....

★ ★ ★

2. Atlantic coastline

   1. In this region,

      (a) the weather will be cold

      (b) there will be clouds in the afternoon

      (c) it will rain

      (d) winds will be moderate

      Which one of these statements is **not** true?

      Write (a), (b), (c) or (d) in the box.

★ ★ ★

3. Brittany – Normandy

   1. What will the weather be like in Brittany in the morning? *(two details)*

      (i)...

      (ii)..

2. In Normandy,

    (a) the morning will be cold

    (b) there will be very few clouds

    (c) there will be some clear spells

    (d) there will be a risk of rain in the early afternoon

    Write (a), (b), (c) or (d) in the box.

3. What minimum temperatures can be expected? ....

★   ★   ★

4. Rhône – Alps

In this region,

    (a) there will be snow at high altitudes in the morning

    (b) it will rain in the valleys

    (c) the afternoon will be cold but cloudy

    (d) temperatures will vary between 0 and 5 degrees

    Write (a), (b), (c) or (d) in the box.

5. La bonne utilisation d'Internet dans un lycée

Marie-Claire and Yves tell us how the Internet is being put to good use in their school.

1. Marie-Claire

1. According to Marie-Claire, what can all students use the school website for?..

2. What are two topics upon which students might like to give their opinion?

   (i)... *recyclage*

   (ii)...

3. Marie-Claire mentions the people of three countries. Name the countries.

   (i)...

   (ii)...

   (iii)...

4. Students can arrange to meet new friends made on the school website

   (a) in the canteen

   (b) in the yard

   (c) at the cinema

   (d) after school

   Write (a), (b), (c) or (d) in the box.

   ★   ★   ★

2. Yves

1. When, according to Yves, might students use the website to buy and sell schoolbooks? ....

2. The website is useful for buying and selling

    (a) CDs

    (b) video games

    (c) a musical instrument

    (d) a mountain bike

    Which one is **not** mentioned by Yves?

    Write (a), (b), (c) or (d) in the box.

3. Yves says that the website can be used to seek help if subjects are causing problems. He mentions two subjects as examples. What are they?

    (i)...

    (ii)...

6. Conseils de révision avant les examens du bac

Madame Renaud, a teacher, talks to Nicole and Gérard to see if they might need help with their exam revision.

1. Madame Renaud talks to Nicole

1. Why has Nicole still not started revision?

    ....

2. Nicole admits that she has spent more time during the year at the cinema than in the library.

    True ☐   False ☐

3. Write down two suggestions that Madame Renaud makes in order to help Nicole:

    (i)...

    (ii)..

4. When should Nicole study difficult subjects?

    ....

5. What, according to Madame Renaud, could Nicole do during breaks from revision work? *(three details)*

    (i)...

    (ii)..

    (iii)...

★ ★ ★

2. Madame Renaud talks to Gérard

1. Why is Gérard working hard at revision?

   ....

2. Gérard explains that he has two problems with his revision work. What are they?

   (i)..

   (ii)...

3. Madame Renaud advises Gérard to concentrate on important points in each subject, such as

   (a) formulae in maths

   (b) dates in history

   (c) ideas in philosophy

   (d) vocabulary and grammar in languages

   Which one does Madame Renaud **not** mention?

   Write (a), (b), (c) or (d) in the box.

4. Madame Renaud advises Gérard to continue to do some physical exercise.

   True ☐   False ☐

7. Le permis de conduire

The day of the driving test has finally arrived for Jean-Yves.

1. How many lessons has Jean-Yves had with the driving school instructor?

    ....

2. His mother accompanied him for several months. He praises her for two qualities. What are they?

    (i)...   (ii) ....

3. What is the date for his driving test? ....

★   ★   ★

4. He spent a sleepless night thinking about

the accelerator		the gears	
the speed limit		the windscreen wipers	
the indicators		the brakes	

    Tick the items that he mentions.

5. What did he adjust, having sat behind the steering wheel?

    ....

★   ★   ★

6. He was asked to turn right, go as far as the roundabout, turn left, and head for the *place Charles de Gaulle.*

   True ☐   False ☐

7. What did he do on the N7? ....

8. Back in town, he was asked to park in front of the post office.

   True ☐   False ☐

   ★   ★   ★

9. The test completed, what did Jean-Yves do? ....

8. L'avenir professionnel

Jérôme and Sylvaine are asked about their career plans.

1. Jérome

1. Next year, Jérôme would like to go to University to study

    (a) arts

    (b) law

    (c) engineering

    (d) sociology

    Write (a), (b), (c) or (d) in the box.

2. After graduation, why would Jérôme like to work in the civil service?
    (two details)

    (i)...

    (ii)..

★   ★   ★

2. Sylvaine

1. Sylvaine would like to work

   (a) in public relations   (c) in computers

   (b) in management   (d) in tourism

   Write (a), (b), (c) or (d) in the box.

2. How long will her period of study last?..

3. What portion of her training takes place in the workplace?

   (a) A quarter   (c) A half

   (b) A third   (d) Two thirds

   Write (a), (b), (c) or (d) in the box.

9. Trois métiers

Three people talk about their jobs.

1. Caroline

1. Where does Caroline work?...
2. How long has she been employed in this type of work?...........................
3. Why does she like her job? ....
4. What advice does she give her customers?...

★   ★   ★

2. Henri

1. What is Henri's job? ....
2. Why does this job suit him perfectly? *(three details)*

    (i)...
    (ii)..
    (iii)...

3. People from three countries work with him. Name the countries.

    (i)..
    (ii)...
    (iii)..

3. Agathe

1. What is Agathe's job? ....

2. How long has she been working with this company? ....

3. What are her working hours?

    Starting time: _____   Finishing time: _____

4. What two languages does she speak fluently?

    (i) .... (ii) ....

10. Travaux à la maison

Sylvie and Pierre are discussing plans to extend their home – first among themselves and then with their architect.

1. Sylvie and Pierre

1. When have they an appointment with the architect?

    (i) Day:...

    (ii) Time: ....

2. What do they intend to do with the garage?

    ....

3. What other plans for the house have they got?

    ....

★　★　★

2. Sylvie and Monsieur Duhamel

1. Why is Pierre not at the architect's office?

    ....

2. What does the architect ask to see?

    ....

3. What question does he put to Sylvie?

    ....

★　★　★

4. How long will it take Monsieur Duhamel to draw up the new plans?

    ....

5. Fill in the missing digits in the telephone number:

02	65		05	

11. Visite en Guadeloupe : vaut le voyage !

Véronique answers questions about the excellent holidays that she had in Guadeloupe.

1. When did Véronique go to Guadeloupe?

   ....

2. Who went with her?

   ....

3. When is the best time of the year to visit Guadeloupe?

   ....

4. Why does Véronique not recommend going there outside of this period? *(two details)*

   (i) .... (ii) ....

5. Why is Guadeloupe an ideal destination for French people going on holidays? *(two details)*

   (i) .... (ii) ....

   ★   ★   ★

6. What aspects of nature are especially beautiful in Guadeloupe? *(two details)*

   (i)..

   (ii)...

7. Write down three activities that they took part in:

   (i)..

   (ii)...

   (iii)..

   ★   ★   ★

8. What problem would you be likely to encounter there in the evening?

    ....

9. How do we know that Véronique was prepared for this problem?

    ....

12. Signes du zodiaque

Listen to the predictions for some star-signs.

1. Aquarius

1. Why is this going to be an important year for Aquarians? *(two details)*

    (i)..

    (ii)...

2. When is it predicted will be the best time of the year for romance?

    ....

★ ★ ★

2. Aries

1. Why will the year start well for people with this star-sign? *(two details)*

    (i)..

    (ii)...

2. Concerning health, what two pieces of advice are given?

    (i)..

    (ii)...

★ ★ ★

3. Capricorn

1. The year will be difficult. Who will help with the problems encountered? *(two details)*

    (i)..

    ....

    (ii)...

    ....

2. What sort of activities are people advised to take part in? *(two details)*

   (i)...

   (ii)..

3. When will be the best time of the year for romance?...............................

13. Des vacances insolites

Sophie and Nicolas have been on unusual holidays.

1. Sophie

1. When did Sophie go on holidays? ....

2. What did she and her family take part in? ....

3. What is the age limit for a child taking part in this activity?

    Lower: ....

    Upper: ....

4. Sophie's mother is very experienced in this sport.

    True [ ]   False [ ]

5. At what age did Sophie start skiing? ....

★   ★   ★

6. Sophie remembered to bring her tennis racket.

    True [ ]   False [ ]

7. Where did the family stay? ....

8. Why did she find the accommodation ideal for the family?

    ....

★   ★   ★

2. Nicolas

1. When did Nicolas go on holidays? ....

2. How long was the holiday? ....

23

3. What did his friends tell him about the scouts? *(three details)*

    (i)...

    (ii)..

    (iii)...

★   ★   ★

4. How did they spend the time during the holidays? *(three details)*

    (i)...

    (ii)..

    (iii)...

5. Where did they sleep the first night? ....

6. Where did they sleep the other nights?..

14. Attention *TRAVAUX* !

Yves and Anne have been invited to their friends' home.

1. Yves and Anne are going to their friends' house

    (a) for a meal

    (b) for a few drinks

    (c) to watch television together

    (d) to discuss holiday plans

    Write (a), (b), (c) or (d) in the box.

2. At what time would Anne expect her mother to arrive? ....

3. Why did Yves think that they would be late in arriving at their friends' house? *(two details)*

    (i)...

    (ii)..

4. What did Anne do while waiting for her mother? *(two details)*

    (i)...

    (ii)..

★   ★   ★

5. What types of vehicles did they notice on the road? *(two details)*

    (i)...

    (ii)..

6. What did the warning notice tell them?

    ....

7. Yves knew that he would have to

    (a) do a u-turn

    (b) phone Jacques and Marie on his mobile phone

    (c) take another road to try to arrive on time

    (d) continue their journey, even if they would be half an hour late

    Write (a), (b), (c) or (d) in the box.

8. Fill in the missing digits in the telephone number:

05		00		15

★   ★   ★

9. What had Marie forgotten to tell Anne?

    ....

le périphérique

se maquiller

quel soulagement!

ralentir

le panneau indicateur

rétrécir

route à voie unique

un bouchon

15. Les informations

You will hear four news items.

1. First news item

Fill in the details of the accident in the grid:

Time	
Place	
Detail about one victim	
Detail about other victim	
Cause of accident	

★   ★   ★

2. Second news item

1. In which city did this incident happen?..

2. At what time did the man escape?..

3. What age was he? ....

4. Why was he in police custody? ....

5. He escaped

   (a) in a stolen car

   (b) in a stolen van

   (c) in a stolen police car

   (d) on a stolen motor-bike

   Write (a), (b), (c) or (d) in the box.

★   ★   ★

3. Third news item

1. Where did this accident take place? ....

2. What age was the man? ....

3. On which part of his body was he burned? ....

4. In a similar accident, two months ago, a young person

   (a) lost an eye

   (b) lost the sight in both eyes

   (c) lost a hand

   (d) lost a leg

   Write (a), (b), (c) or (d) in the box.

4. Fourth news item

1. Which country has the highest life expectancy? ....

2. What is the population of that country? ....

3. What are the two main items of their diet?

   (i) ....

   (ii) ....

16. Attention aux jeux informatiques

A young French person admits that he spends too much time playing with computer games.

1. When did Serge begin playing computer games?..

2. How did he become interested in them? ....

3. What is the name that he uses in the games? ....

4. In the games, what is he always trying to do? *(two details)*

    (i)...

    (ii)..

★ ★ ★

5. What is his favourite game at the moment?

    ....

6. How many hours per week does he spend at these games?

    ....

7. His parents make three complaints about him. What are they?

    (i)...

    (ii)..

    (iii)...

8. Tick the items that the interviewer mentions at
    the end:

School work	✓	Family	
Career		Exam results	
Sleep	✓	Health	

17. Les jeunes et le bénévolat

Benoît is deeply concerned about social issues.

1. Why did Benoît first take an interest in social issues?

   ....

2. Whom does he help? ....

3. How many times per week does he take part in this work?

   ....

4. What exactly does he do? ....

5. Why are the children slow to cooperate at first? *(two details)*

   (i)..

   (ii)...

6. What does he do to get their attention? *(two details)*

   (i)..

   (ii)...

   ★   ★   ★

7. What age is Benoît's cousin? ....

8. What work does he do in prisons? ....

9. How much time per week does he give to this work? ....

18. Les flash-mobs, le tout dernier phénomène

Pascal tells his teacher about the latest craze!

1. According to Pascal, how many people would take part in a *flash-mob*?

    (a) Several

    (b) About a dozen

    (c) A hundred

    (d) Hundreds

    Write (a), (b), (c) or (d) in the box.

2. What would the e-mail tell him? *(two details)*

    (i).. (ii) ....

3. Details of a *flash-mob* are known well in advance.

    True ⬜   False ⬜

    ★   ★   ★

4. In which city does Pascal live?...

5. In that city, what did the participants in a *flash-mob* do? *(three details)*

    (i)..

    (ii)...

    (iii)...

6. What was their aim? ....

    ★   ★   ★

7. Where, in New York, did a *flash-mob* take place? ....

8. They tried to imitate the sounds of animals. Which three animals are mentioned?

   (i)...

   (ii)...

   (iii)...

19. Les prévisions météorologiques

You will hear the weather forecast for four days.

1. Saturday

Write one weather detail for each area in the grid:

North of the Loire	
From the South-West to the Alps	
Near the Mediterranean	

★   ★   ★

2. Sunday

1. Describe the weather in the South-East. *(two details)*

    (i)...

    (ii)..

2. In Aquitaine, the weather will be overcast and wet.

    True ☐   False ☐

3. Where will there be clear spells?...

★   ★   ★

3. Monday

1. What will the weather in the West be like? *(two details)*

    (i)...

    (ii)..

2. Where will it be sunny? ....

★   ★   ★

4. Tuesday

1. What will Tuesday's weather be like? *(two details)*

    (i)...

    (ii)..

2. What temperatures can be expected?..

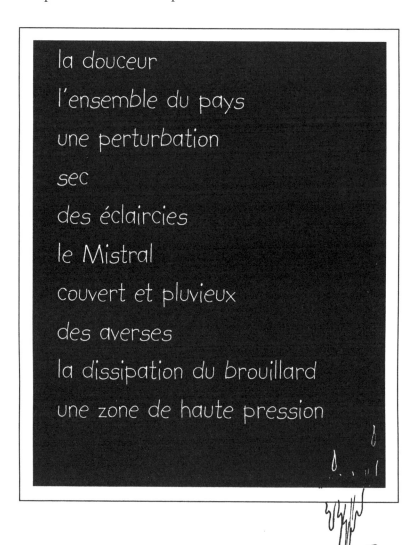

la douceur

l'ensemble du pays

une perturbation

sec

des éclaircies

le Mistral

couvert et pluvieux

des averses

la dissipation du brouillard

une zone de haute pression

20. Reconcilier petit boulot et études, est-ce possible ?

Is it possible to have a part-time job and study? A career guidance counsellor and three students will give their opinions.

1. Monsieur Lebrun

1. In which circumstance would Monsieur Lebrun agree that a student could have a job?

   ....

2. What does he say is a key factor for success in study?

   ....

★   ★   ★

2. Elsa

1. What is Elsa's part-time job? ....

2. How often does she work?...

3. What does she use the money for? *(two details)*

   (i)..

   (ii)...

★   ★   ★

3. Marc

1. What does Marc study?...

2. What does he use the money for? *(three details)*

   (i)..

   (ii)...

   (iii)..

3. What problem does he have?..

★   ★   ★

4. Véronique

1. What does Véronique say about her parents? *(two details)*

    (i)...

    (ii)..

2. Where does she work during the summer holidays?

    ....

21. Rêvons nos vacances

Will there be a life after the *baccalauréat*? Listen to the views of four students.

1. Pauline

1. When does Pauline dream of the holidays?

    ....

2. With whom is she going to go camping? ....

3. Which subject is she studying at the moment? ....

★   ★   ★

2. Roland

1. What job will Roland have in July?..

2. What will he do with the money he gets?

    ....

3. Where will he stay?...

★   ★   ★

3. Zoé

1. On what condition will Zoé's parents give her a ticket to go to the United States of America?

    ....

2. What will she do in New York?

  (a) Work

  (b) Study

  (c) Meet her boyfriend

  (d) Hire a car

   Write (a), (b), (c) or (d) in the box.

★   ★   ★

4. Jean–Claude

1. What will Jean-Claude help to renovate? ....

2. In which French region will he be working?...

3. What will he do to relax afterwards? ....

4. What subject is he revising at the moment?..

22. A quoi servent les langues et les maths ?

Students are discussing the importance of languages and maths. Listen to two conversations.

1. Marie and Julien

1. Which three languages does Marie mention?

    (i)..

    (ii)...

    (iii)..

2. Which language does Julien hope to study at University? ....

3. According to Marie, why should we study the languages of the countries of Eastern Europe?

    ....

4. What is the last language that Julien mentions?......................................

★ ★ ★

2. Claire and Robin

1. Claire accuses Robin of being interested only in

    (a) numbers

    (b) sport

    (c) chemistry

    (d) exam results

    Write (a), (b), (c) or (d) in the box.

2. Robin tells Claire that he would like to be a sound engineer.

    True ☐   False ☐

3. Which subjects does Claire include in her list?

    (i)..   (iii)..

    (ii)...   (iv)..

23. Les informations

You will hear three news stories and a weather forecast.

1. First news item

1. ~~What percentage~~ of international sports federations have adopted the code which bans the use ~~of drugs in sport?~~

   ....

2. As well as football and cycling, what are the other sports which are accused of dragging their feet?

   (i)...

   (ii)...

   (iii)...

3. What term of suspension is to be imposed on athletes who have been found to have taken banned substances?

   ....

★   ★   ★

2. Second news item

Fill in the details of the accident in the grid:

Number of women killed	2
Age of women	27 21
Time	Saturday morning
Place	A13 motorway - Paris
Cause of accident	Another motorist 27 -who was driving fast

★   ★   ★

3. Third news item

1. What offence did the young couple commit?

    ....

2. On what special day in the year did they commit the offence?

    ....

3. How were they travelling?...

4. How much were they fined?..

    Conditional.
5. What could they have bought for the amount of the fine? *(two details)*

    (i)...

    (ii)..

★ ★ ★

4. Weather forecast

1. What will the weather be like in the early afternoon?

    ....

2. Describe the weather in Corsica. *(two details)*

    (i)...

    (ii)..

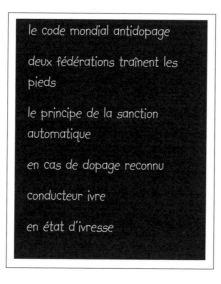

le code mondial antidopage

deux fédérations traînent les pieds

le principe de la sanction automatique

en cas de dopage reconnu

conducteur ivre

en état d'ivresse

24. En panne

Fabrice and Sophie are setting out for a drive.

1. What is the weather like as they set off? ....

2. Why does Fabrice want to leave promptly? ....

★　★　★

3. How many kilometres have they travelled when Fabrice thinks he can smell the sea?

   ....

4. What is the problem with the car?

   ....

5. What has Fabrice forgotten to bring? ....

★　★　★

6. How long will they have to wait for the breakdown truck to arrive?

   ....

7. Where does Sophie imagine that they may now be forced to have their picnic? *(two possibilities)*

   (i)..

   (ii)...

25. La météo

The weather forecast will give details for today in France.

1. Write down the times:

   Sunrise: ....

   Sunset: ....

2. Which part of the country will be sunny for most of the day?

   ....

3. What temperatures can be expected in that area in the afternoon?

   ....

★ ★ ★

4. Write down two weather details for the Centre of France:

   (i)..

   (ii)...

5. What will the minimum temperature be in the Centre? ....

6. What will the maximum temperature be in the Centre?...........................

7. In the final regions mentioned, what will the weather be like in the morning?

   ....

8. What can be expected in the afternoon? ....

26. Une bonne soirée

Some young people are discussing what they may do to amuse themselves.

1. Muriel and Aurélie

1. According to Muriel, what is happening on Saturday evening?

   ....

2. Why is Aurélie not keen to go out this weekend?

   ....

3. What does Aurélie intend to do at home? *(two details)*

   (i)...

   (ii)..

★   ★   ★

4. With whom will Muriel go out instead? ....

★   ★   ★

2. Patrick and Jules

1. Patrick greets Jules and tells him that he is tired of having to study.

   True ⬜   False ⬜

2. How long has it been since they played chess?..

3. What does Jules say that he will bring to eat? ....

4. Why would Jules like to bring Julie? ....

5. Why does Patrick say 'no' to that request?

   ....

27. En bref

You will hear three news items and a weather forecast.

1. First news item

1. What age is the girl? ....

2. Over what issue did she have to leave her old school?

   ....

3. The teachers in her new school are threatening

   (a) to put the girl in detention

   (b) to have the girl expelled from the school

   (c) to write to her parents about the problem

   (d) to go on strike

   Write (a), (b), (c) or (d) in the box.

★　★　★

2. Second news item

1. What has the Road Safety Agency announced?

   ....

2. When did they make this announcement?..

3. On what period of the year was the result of their survey based?

   ....

★　★　★

3. Third news item

1. How many people have been put in prison?...

2. In which French city did this occur? ....

45

3. What did the police discover in the apartment? *(two details)*

   (i)..

   (ii)...

4. Of which country was one of the men a native?

   ....

★   ★   ★

4. Weather Forecast

Fill in the details in the grid:

Weather for France	
Weather for Germany	
Weather for North Africa	

28. Les Jeux olympiques

First you will hear an account of the Olympic Games returning to their place of origin.

You will then hear a conversation in which two people discuss the Games.

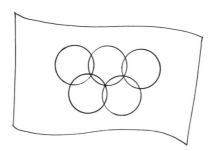

1. What contradictory aspect does Athens possess?

   ....

2. Holding the Games, what does the city of Athens wish to show the world?

   ....

   ★   ★   ★

3. In the ancient Games, taking part was as important as winning.

   True ☐   False ☐

   ★   ★   ★

4. Why does Jean-Claude feel that he will be doing something similar to the ancient Greeks?

   ....

5. What three sports does Anne hope to see?

   (i)...

   (ii)..

   (iii)...

6. What, according to Anne and Jean-Claude, would spoil the Games?

   ....

29. Pas de sorties !

Life is difficult for students. Two conversations will tell you why!

1. Paul and Julie

1. Where does Paul no longer have time to go? *(two details)*

    (i)..

    (ii)...

2. Where is the supermarket in which he works situated?

    ....

3. When does he train for football? ....

4. When does he intend to give up his job?..

★　★　★

2. Véronique and Pierre

1. When do Véronique's parents want her to start revision for her exams?

    ....

2. When do Pierre's parents get annoyed? ....

3. For what items does Pierre claim that his parents have difficulty in finding the money? *(two details)*

    (i)..

    (ii)...

4. Véronique says that parents have no difficulty in finding money for something. What is it? ....

30. Une belle tradition

Jules is talking with his grandmother.

1. What does Jules say that his grandmother is in the habit of saying?

   ....

2. On what date is the feast of the Epiphany celebrated? ....

3. According to Jules, what does his mother do to prepare for the feast?

   ....

4. According to grandmother, what used they do in the old days which was different to today?

   ....

★ ★ ★

5. What could the person who got the « fève » choose?...............................

6. How used they finish the evening?..

L'épiphanie

les rois mages

la galette des rois

un santon

le roi

la reine

31. Paris en roller

Bénédicte talks about roller-blading, the latest craze to hit the streets of Paris.

1. On which evening of the week does the special session for roller-bladers take place? ....

2. On what two conditions can one take part in this session?

   (i)...

   (ii)..

3. What time of the week is set aside for beginners?

   ....

★ ★ ★

4. Where did Bénédicte and the others go roller-blading last Friday evening?

   ....

5. You must always roller-blade on the footpath, and never on the road.

   True ☐   False ☐

6. If a person falls, it can cause

   (a) a pile-up

   (b) an argument

   (c) a fight

   (d) a major accident

   Write (a), (b), (c) or (d) in the box. ☐

32. Bizarre ... mais vrai !

1. What claim does the person living in Wisconsin make?

    ....

2. Over what period of time has his wife put on a lot of weight?

    ....

3. What does he say about his children?

    ....

★   ★   ★

4. In what way does he say that his own behaviour has changed? *(two details)*

    (i)...

    (ii)...

5. What would he need to be given in exchange for abandoning his claim for compensation? *(three details)*

    (i)...

    (ii)...

    (iii)..

33. Les informations

You will hear three news items and a weather forecast.

1. First news item

   1. At what time did the accident take place?...

   2. Where did it occur? ....

   3. What are we told about the two victims?

      (i)...

      (ii)..

★   ★   ★

2. Second news item

   1. In which city did the incident occur?.......................................

   2. When did it happen? ....

   3. What age was the man?..

   4. What was he accused of?..

   5. How did he make his escape?...

★   ★   ★

3. Third news item

   1. This strike will involve

      (a) trains

      (b) banks

      (c) post-offices

      (d) schools

      Write (a), (b), (c) or (d) in the box.   □

   2. When will the strike take place?...

   3. How long will it last?...

4. What is the reason for the strike? ....

★   ★   ★

4. Weather forecast

1. What is the outlook for tomorrow? *(two details)*

    (i)...

    (ii)..

2. The morning will be misty and foggy.

    True ☐   False ☐

3. Temperatures will remain the same.

    True ☐   False ☐

34. La publicité

Two people will give opinions about advertising.

1. Clément Jazot

1. Why does Clément say that he hates advertising?

    ....

2. Tick the items that are mentioned:

Trucks		Radio	
Walls		Cinema	
Bus shelters		Television	
Public transport		Kitchen presses	
Letter-boxes		Newspapers	

    ★   ★   ★

3. What proportion of advertising signs is illegal? ....

4. What does Clément suggest that people might do to show opposition to advertising? *(two details)*

    (i)...

    (ii)..

    ★   ★   ★

2. Marine Javelle

1. Why is Marine in favour of advertising?

    ....

2. Marine does not agree with a certain point of view. What is it?

    ....

    ★   ★   ★

3. She mentions three types of advertisement. What are they?

   (i)...

   (ii)..

   (iii)..

35. Quelles vacances !

Four friends had an eventful skiing holiday. Listen to an account of what happened?

1. In which month did the four friends go on holidays? ....

2. In which city do they live? ....

3. How did they get to the skiing resort? ....

4. At what time did they set out? ....

★   ★   ★

5. How long was the journey expected to take? ....

6. What happened on the way? ....

★   ★   ★

7. What slope was Luc descending when he fell? ....

8. What injury did he sustain? ....

9. What did Luc want his three friends to do?

   ....

10. What was their decision? ....

36. Le réchauffement climatique

A meteorologist talks about the worrying problem of global warming.

1. How many people died in France during the heatwave of early August last year?

    ....

2. It is forecast that, between now and 2100, temperatures will increase by 2 to 6 degrees.

    True ☐   False ☐

    ★   ★   ★

3. Tick the items that are mentioned:

    A rise in the level of the sea   ☐

    Warmer summers   ☐

    Milder and wetter winters   ☐

    More frequent forest fires   ☐

    ★   ★   ★

4. What two solutions are proposed to try to reduce the increase in temperatures?

    (i)..

    (ii)..

37. Les 35 heures

The length of the working week is being reduced. Two people give opposing views on this.

1. Stéphanie

1. What is Stéphanie's job?..

2. How many hours per week used she work before the reduction?

....

★ ★ ★

3. What does she do now to benefit from the extra free time? *(four details)*

(i)...

(ii)..

(iii)...

(iv)...

★ ★ ★

2. Marc

1. Where does Marc work?..

2. Marc says that he preferred the old working week. Write down two reasons why he dislikes the present working arrangements:

(i)...

(ii)..

3. What used he be able to do in the old system which he can no longer do?

....

38. Une famille victime des inondations

Madame Peyre has very unpleasant memories of the floods which devastated the town.

1. The town was flooded on three occasions. Write the dates in the grid:

First flood	
Second flood	
Third flood	

2. Which was the worst of these floods and why?

    ....

3. For how long was she and her family out of their home?..........................

4. Write down four details of what they lost in the flood:

    (i)..

    (ii)...

    (iii)..

    (iv)..

    ★   ★   ★

5. Where was the children's bedroom? ....

6. The children

(a) were asleep when the water entered the house

(b) escaped through the window

(c) knew that the house was being flooded

(d) managed to open their bedroom window before escaping

Write (a), (b), (c) or (d) in the box.

39. Les sports

You will hear news from three sports.

1. Golf

Write the amount earned by each sports person in the grid:

Tiger Woods	
Michael Schumacher	
David Beckham	

★   ★   ★

2. Tennis

1. What decision has been made by the organisers of the Wimbledon Tournament?

    ....

2. By what date do they hope that this work will be completed?

    ....

★   ★   ★

3. Cycling

1. When did Bettini win the race? ....

2. In which country did the race take place? ....

3. Write down the names of two other countries in which he was victorious this year:

    (i)..   (ii) ....

40. Il y a vacances et ... vacances

Four young French people describe their holidays.

1. Jean-Pierre

1. With whom does Jean-Pierre spend his holidays? ....

2. Which month do they spend in the villa?...

3. Write down three things that he says about their holidays:

    (i)...

    (ii)..

    (iii)...

★   ★   ★

2. Pauline

1. Why does Pauline dislike family holidays?

    ....

2. What does she like to do when on holiday? *(three details)*

    (i)...

    (ii)..

    (iii)...

3. For Pauline, what is the most important thing about going on holidays?

    ....

★   ★   ★

3. Pierric

1. How does Pierric like to travel when going on holidays?...........................

2. What does he like to do on holiday? *(three details)*

    (i)..

    (ii)...

    (iii)..

3. What three languages does he speak?

    (i)..

    (ii)...

    (iii)..

★ ★ ★

4. Anne

1. Why will Anne not be going on holidays this summer? ....

2. Where exactly does she hope to go next year?...

3. She will be going there for

    (a) the culture
    (b) the language
    (c) the fine weather
    (d) the food

    Write (a), (b), (c) or (d) in the box.

41. Des vacances en Irlande

Alice has spent a holiday in Ireland. She describes her experience.

1. Who came with Alice to Ireland? ....

2. What did they do at the airport? ....

3. How does she describe Connemara? *(three details)*

     (i) ....

     (ii) ....

     (iii) ....

4. Write down one thing that they did while in Connemara:

     ....

★ ★ ★

5. What does she say about Clifden? *(two details)*

     (i) ....

     (ii) ....

6. What did they do after leaving Clifden *(three details)*

     (i) ....

     (ii) ....

     (iii) ....

7. What remarkable feature of the Irish weather did she notice?

     ....

42. Un accident sur les pistes

Listen to an account of how a young girl was injured while on a skiing holiday.

1. What age was the girl? ....

2. Fill in the details in the grid:

Who was with her?	
Day	
Time of accident	

★   ★   ★

3. The girl was injured

   (a) when she fell on the ski-slopes

   (b) when another skier collided with her

   (c) when she got stuck in the ski-lift

   (d) when an avalanche swept down the mountain

   Write (a), (b), (c) or (d) in the box.

4. What were her injuries? *(two details)*

   (i)

   (ii)

43. Mon séjour à Dublin

Thomas had a very enjoyable holiday in Dublin. Back in France, he reflects on his experience.

1. How many friends came with Thomas to Dublin?

    ....

2. How long did they spend here?..

3. Fill in the details about their flight:

Name of French airport	
Cost of tickets	
Method of reservation	

★ ★ ★

4. What struck him about Dublin? *(two details)*

    (i)..

    (ii)...

5. According to Thomas, what is the best way to see the Irish capital?

   ....

6. What did he do during the day?

   ....

7. What did he do in the evenings? *(two details)*

   (i)...
   (ii)..

44. Des vacances ratées

Rémi and Laure are about to go on holidays. But there's a problem.

1. How did Laure find out about the problem? ....

2. Who in the airline industry are going on strike?

    (a) Pilots

    (b) Air stewards

    (c) Baggage handlers

    (d) Air control staff

    Write (a), (b), (c) or (d) in the box.

3. Which two airports could be affected?

    (i)...

    (ii)..

4. When, according to Rémi, do they always seem to choose to go on strike?

    ....

    ★   ★   ★

5. What are the two things that Laure is hoping for when they arrive at their ski-resort?

    (i)...

    (ii)..

45. D'autres langues en France que le français

Pauline speaks *occitan*, one of France's regional languages.

Parlez-vous occitan?

1. Where in France does Pauline live? ....

2. Pauline says that *occitan* is a mixture of three languages. What are they?

   (i)...

   (ii)...

   (iii)...

3. In which century did this language originate? ....

4. Who used the language until the sixteenth century?

....

★ ★ ★

5. Where can one learn *occitan* today?

....

6. Which two regional languages are more widely spoken than *occitan*?

   (i)...

   (ii)...

7. What is Pauline's opinion on the importance of regional languages?

....

46. Les carrières

People are discussing choice of career.

1. Sébastien and Monique

1. What is Sébastien's choice of career? ....

2. Why does Monique say that she will not choose to study medicine to be a doctor?

    ....

3. What career will she choose instead? ....

★   ★   ★

2. Bernard and Jérôme

1. What aspect of Bernard's schoolwork does his French teacher praise?

    ....

2. What job would he like to have? ....

3. Why would Jérôme like to become a helicopter pilot? ....

    ....

★   ★   ★

3. Agnès and Laure

1. What job would Laure like to have? ....

2. What kind of shop would Agnès like to open?

    ....

47. La mode des piercings et des tatouages

Having a piercing or a tattoo is all the rage in France. You will hear some statistics, and then an interview with Karine.

1. Fill in the percentages in the grid:

Teenagers who have a piercing or tattoo	%
Parents who disapprove	%

2. What do sociologists say about the matter?

....

★ ★ ★

3. In which part of her body did Karine have the most recent piercing?

....

4. What was she forced to do for a week after getting it? *(three details)*

(i)...

(ii)..

(iii)...

★ ★ ★

5. What do her parents say about it?

....

6. Why is Karine very much in favour of this fashion? *(two details)*

(i)...

(ii)..

48. La météo

You will hear weather forecast details for a number of days.

1. Tomorrow

1. From Normandy to the Massif-Central, what will be the feature of tomorrow's weather?

   ....

2. What is forecast for the Mediterranean region?

   ....

★   ★   ★

2. The day after tomorrow

Fill in the details in the grid:

North	
South	
Atlantic coast	

★   ★   ★

3. Saturday and Sunday

1. What is forecast for the morning throughout the country?

   ....

2. What will the weather be like later in the day from the North to the Vosges Mountains?

   ....

3. What type of weather is forecast for the Centre and the South?

   ....

49. A la recherche d'un logement

Gérard has met Amélie in the street. He tells her about his search for an apartment.

1. Why has Gérard been forced to live with his parents up until now?

   ....

2. What good news did he receive last week?

   ....

3. What type of apartment is he looking for? *(three details)*

   (i)...

   (ii)..

   (iii)...

★   ★   ★

4. What is special about the apartment which he has just seen? *(three details)*

   (i)...

   (ii)..

   (iii)...

5. How much per month would he be willing to pay for it?.........................

6. What request does Amélie put to Gérard at the end?

   ....

73

50. Le téléphone portable : ses avantages et inconvénients

Madame Langlois and Madame Berger are a bit dubious about the merits of mobile phones!

1. How many children has Madame Langlois? ....

2. To whom do young people like to send text-messages?

    ....

3. For what reason did Madame Berger's children offer to buy her a phone at Christmas?

    ....

★ ★ ★

4. What particularly annoys Madame Berger about mobile phones?

    ....

5. What has she already done that makes her reluctant to try to ban mobile phones in her home?

    ....

51. Coup de téléphone

Juliette gets a telephone call from her friend, Geoffrey.

1. Geoffrey phones Juliette because

    (a) he wants to invite her out on Saturday

    (b) he wants to show her his new apartment

    (c) he needs some help as he's moving to his new apartment

    (d) he would like her to help him decorate his new apartment

    Write (a), (b), (c) or (d) in the box.

2. Why does Geoffrey like the area in which he lives? *(three details)*

    (i)..

    (ii)...

    (iii)..

    ★   ★   ★

3. Write down three reasons why he likes his new apartment:

    (i)..

    (ii)...

    (iii)..

4. How much is the rent?..

5. At what time should Juliette arrive? ....

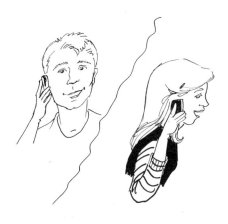

52. Un métier commun ... et une autre vie

At a school in the Vendée region, pupils ask their teachers about their interests outside of school. You will hear the replies of three teachers.

1. Madame Poncet

1. What subject does Madame Poncet teach? ....

2. She likes reading. What does she read? *(four details)*

    (i)..   (iii) ....

    (ii)...   (iv) ....

3. What is her second interest? ....

4. How do we know that she is very dedicated to this interest? *(two details)*

    (i)...

    (ii)..

★   ★   ★

2. Monsieur Loriol

1. What subject does Monsieur Loriol teach? ....

2. What is his great interest? ....

3. Which countries has he already visited?

    (i)...

    (ii)..

4. For how long has he been practising yoga? ....

3. Madame Cambon

1. What does Madame Cambon teach? ....

2. What is her hobby? ....

3. Where does she like to take up her position when engaged in this interest?
    (two details)

    (i) ....   (ii) ....

53. Des idées de voyage

Maybe you might like some ideas for an unforgettable holiday?

1. Bulgaria

1. For what kind of holiday is Bulgaria recommended?

   ....

2. How long is the aeroplane flight from Paris? ....

3. Fill in the prices in the grid:

Seven nights in a four-star hotel	€
Airport taxes	€
Two weeks in the same hotel	€

★   ★   ★

2. Malaga

1. What event made Malaga important as a destination for cultural holidays?

   ....

2. The town is much more lively in summer than in winter.

   True [ ]   False [ ]

3. What would you get for €400? *(two details)*

   (i)...

   (ii)..

4. Where would your hotel be situated? ....

5. Until what date is this offer available? ....

54. Handicap : immersion dans le monde du silence

Léa talks to Jean-Pierre about an interesting exhibition that she attended.

1. With whom did Léa go to the exhibition? ....

2. For how long did she experience the 'world of silence'? ....

3. What did she put on when she entered the exhibition room?

   ....

★   ★   ★

4. Where did the guide bring her? ....

5. How did she communicate? ....

6. Until when is the exhibition open? ....

55. Une étude des accidents de la route

An expert on road safety speaks about the results of his recent survey.

1. According to Monsieur Caban, what proportion of road accidents could be avoided?

   ....

2. What do some motorists forget to check? ....

3. In what circumstances do some drivers drive too fast? *(two details)*

   (i)..

   (ii)...

★ ★ ★

4. When, according to Monsieur Caban, does a road accident most frequently occur?

   ....

5. What do the most stupid drivers do? *(three details)*

   (i)..

   (ii)...

   (iii)..

6. What does a driver often believe?...

56. Planète web

Aurélie and Thomas talk about the Internet.

1. What did Thomas do on his computer the previous evening?

    ....

2. How long did Aurélie spend 'surfing the net'? ....

3. What did she find there? ....

★   ★   ★

4. What kind of cooking does Thomas prefer? ....

5. Write down one of the recipes that he found on a website:

    ....

6. When does Thomas want Aurélie to come to his place for a meal?

    ....

57. Les conséquences des grandes chaleurs

The summer heatwave has caused many problems. Listen to an account of three of them.

1. First problem

1. How many people died in Paris because of the intense heat?

   ....

2. Which two categories of people are most at risk?

   (i)...

   (ii)..

3. What other problem does the heat bring? ....

★ ★ ★

2. Second problem

1. In which two regions have forest fires occurred?

    (i)...

    (ii)...

2. What special equipment did firefighters use? ....

3. What did people in some villages do?...

★ ★ ★

3. Third problem

Fill in the details in the grid:

Reason why mountains are dangerous	
Number of people rescued	
Day on which this happened	
Police action taken as a result	

58. Les traditions se perdent-elles ?

Are the old traditions surviving in France?

1. What is the date of the Feast of the Epiphany? ....

2. Write down two things that people do on Shrove Tuesday:

   (i)...

   (ii)..

3. What do children talk about at Easter?

   ....

4. It's a free day for everybody! What date is it? ....

5. On which date does everybody go to the beach for a picnic?

   ....

6. What happens at Hallowe'en?

   ....

★　★　★

7. Write down the names of four other special days:

   (i)   ....   (iii) ....

   (ii) ....   (iv) ....

59. A la recherche d'un travail

Patrick is about to look for a job. He needs some advice on how to write his CV.

1. According to the person whom Patrick consults, what are the distinguishing features of a good CV? *(two details)*

    (i)...

    (ii)..

★　★　★

2. On the question of languages, what is Patrick advised to put on his CV? *(two details)*

    (i)...

    (ii)..

3. Which two languages does Patrick speak?

    (i)...

    (ii)..

4. How long did Patrick spend in England?...

★　★　★

5. What sport does Patrick play? ....

6. According to the adult, what will the mention of sport on a CV prove?

    ....

7. What kind of photograph should Patrick include with his CV? *(two details)*

    (i)...

    (ii)..

60. Les grandes causes

Jacques Renaud is a young man living in Paris. He is very committed to the fight against social problems.

1. Fill in the details in the grid:

Year that *Attac* was set up	
Number of countries in which it exists	
Problems that it fights against	(i)
	(ii)
	(iii)
	(iv)

★   ★   ★

2. According to Jacques Renaud, what does the participation of young people add to a protest?

    ....

3. Where did the protest picnics take place? ....

4. What did the protestors eat and drink? *(three details)*

    (i)...

    (ii)..

    (iii)...

5. What did this protest set out to show?..

61. Claude Monet

Listen to an account of the life of Claude Monet.

1. In which year was Claude Monet born?...

2. In which city did he spend his childhood? ....

3. What subjects did Boudin teach him how to paint? *(four details)*

    (i)...   (iii) ....

    (ii)...   (iv) ....

4. What did he do at the age of 20? ....

★   ★   ★

5. In which year did Monet go to live in Giverny?...

6. What did he have built in his garden?...

★   ★   ★

7. At what time did Monet use to get up? ....

8. Why did he take walks in his garden?...

9. What did the people of Giverny think of him?

    ....

62. James Joyce

James Joyce, the famous novelist, spent 20 years of his life in Paris.

1. In what year was James Joyce born?...

2. What information are we given about his father? *(two details)*

    (i)...

    (ii)...

3. In what way would James become like his father?

    ....

★   ★   ★

4. As well as writing, what else was Joyce interested in?

    ....

5. In which year did he leave Dublin? ....

★   ★   ★

6. Fill in the years:

    Arrival in Paris:...

    Publication of *Ulysses*: ....

7. From what did James Joyce draw his inspiration?

    ....